The Battle of Moytura

or,

The First Battle of Mag Tuired

H.2.17 (T.C.D.)

I. 'Children of powerful Nemed, what is the cause of your assembling? What has brought you here—contest, conflict, or combat?'

'What has brought us from our homes, wise Fintan, is this: we suffer at the hands of the Fomorians of Ireland by reason of the greatness of the tribute.'

'Whatever be the tribute, on whomsoever and wheresoever imposed, it is in our power either to bear it or to escape from it.

'There is among you a party, quarrelsome though few in all the land, that do more to ruin it than the tribute of the Fomorians.

'Depart if you feel the time is ripe, glorious sons of Nemed; do not suffer wrong, remain not here, but go far hence.'

2. 'Is that your advice to us, wise Fintan?' 'It is,' said Fintan, 'and I have yet more counsel for you: you must not go by one route or in one direction, for a fleet cannot be brought together without outbreak of fighting; a large number means quarrelling, strangers provoke challenge, and an armed host conflict. You do not find it easy to live together in any one spot in Ireland, and it would not be any easier for your hosts in seeking new homes.

3. 'Depart from this land, children of Nemed; leave Ireland, and escape the violence of your enemies.

'Stay here no longer, pay no more tribute. Your sons or your grandsons will recover the land from which you are now fleeing.

'You shall travel to the land of the Greeks—'tis no lying tale I tell—and though you set out in thousands, your strength will not be found sufficient in the East.

'The children of steadfast Beothach shall leave you and go towards the cold North, the children of Semeon to the East though you feel it strange, depart.'

4. So they parted from each other, Fintan and the famous children of Nemed. Beothach, son of Iarbonel, remained, with his ten men and their wives, in Ireland, according to the poet:

Iarbonel's son, Beothach of the clear-spoken judgments, remained in Ireland. His children went far eastward, to the north-west of Lochlann.

5. Astonishing is the ignorance shown by those who would have it that Tait, son of Tabarn, was sole king over the children of Nemed, for he was yet unborn. He was born in the East, and never came to Ireland.

6. Immense was the fleet, eager the gathering_considering from how few sprang the great company that set out from Ireland, for only thirty men had escaped at the taking of Conaing's Tower, and of these a third remained with Beothach in Ireland. The remaining twenty must have multiplied greatly, for the number of ships that were now leaving Ireland was ten thousand, one hundred and forty.

Those dear friends, then, separated, and sad and sorrowful was the little remnant that remained in Ireland. . .

7. ...the mysteries of wizardry, the knowledge, learning, and prophetic powers, the mastery of arms and skill in cunning feats, the travels and wanderings of the sons of Ibath, for it happened that those tales that had all gone abroad from one place came to be told. A different narrative is necessary for each race. Touching the children of Semeon, son of Starn. A storm had driven them from their course till they came to the dry strands of Thrace and the sandy shores of Greece, and there they settled. Thereupon the

inhabitants and the champions of the land visited them, and made a compact of peace and concord with them. Territory was apportioned them, but on the sea-shore, on the distant borders, on cold rough stretches and rugged rocks, on the hill-sides and mountain slopes, on inhospitable heights and in deep ravines, on broken land and ground unfit for cultivation. But the strangers transported a great quantity of soil to the smooth, bare rocks, and made them into smiling clover-covered plains.

8. When the chiefs and powerful men of the land saw the smooth, broad and grassy fields, and the wide expanses of fruitful cultivated land, they would expel the occupants, and give them in exchange wild, rugged regions, hard stony lands infested with poisonous serpents. However, they tamed and cultivated the ground, and made it into good fruitful fields, smooth and broad like all their land that was taken from them.

9. But in the meantime the children of Nemed increased and multiplied till they numbered many thousands. The tribute grew heavier and their labour harder till they, now a powerful company, resolved secretly to make wide curved boats of the well-woven bags they used for carrying soil, and to sail for Ireland.

10. Two hundred years had passed since the taking of Conaing's Tower till the return of the children of Semeon to Ireland. It was at the same time that the famous warlike children of Israel were leaving Egypt in search of the happy land of promise, while the descendants of Gaidel Glas moved up from the south after the escape of the people of God and the drowning of Pharaoh, and came to cold, rugged Scythia.

11. During the two hundred years after the taking of Conaing's Tower the children of Semeon multiplied till they numbered many thousands, forming strong bold hosts. On account of the severity of the labour and the heaviness of the bondage imposed

on them they determined to flee from persecution, endeavour to escape and make their way to Ireland.

12. They made boats of their sacks, and stole some of the vessels, boats, and galleys of the soldiers of the Greeks. The lords and leaders, heads, chiefs and champions of that fleet were the five sons of Dela, according to the poet:

To noble Ireland there set out the five sons of Dela son of Loth the impetuous, Rudraige, Genann, Gann, Slainge of the spears, and Sengann.

13. They made off at nightfall, and manned their ships in the harbour where they had first landed. Slainge, the elder of the company, who was judge among his brothers, harangued them as follows:

'Now is the time for exertion, care, and watchfulness; fierce and grey with foam is the sea; each fair fleet sets forth to escape from intolerable wrong; the tyranny of the Greeks is unaccustomed; the plains of salmon-bearing Ireland we must strive to win. 'Give heed to and observe the wrong and injustice you suffer. You have in us five good men to lead the fleet, each of us a match for a hundred.'

'That is true,' his followers replied. 'Let us make the people of this land pay in full for the servitude and the heavy tribute they imposed on us.' And so they killed every one of the Greeks worth killing that they got hold of, and wasted the neighbouring land and made a devastating incursion over it and burnt it. They then brought their plunder and spoil to the place where their ships and galleys were and the smooth, black-prowed boats they had made of their sacks and bags, that is, to Traig Tresgad.

14.One thousand one hundred and thirty was the number of ships that put out, according to the poet:

'One thousand one hundred and thirty ships—that, without falsehood, is the number that accompanied Genann and his people from the East.

Numerous, indeed, were the Fir Boig when they left Greece, a stout company that set out vigorously on their voyage, but not in a fleet built of wood.

On Wednesday they put out to the West over the wide Tyrrhenian sea, and after a period of a full year and three days they arrived in Spain.'

From there to noble Ireland they made a speedy voyage; all may proclaim it, they took a period of thirteen days.'

15. So they came to Spain. They asked of their seers and druids for information and direction concerning the winds which should next carry them to Ireland. They sailed onwards before a south-west wind till they saw Ireland in the distance. But at that point the wind rose high and strong, and its violence drove huge waves against the sides of the ships; and the fleet separated into three great divisions, the Gaileoin, the Fir Boig and the Fir Domnann. Slainge put to shore at Inber Slainge in the fifth of the Gaileoin; Rudraige landed at Tracht Rudraige in Ulster; and Genann in Inber Domnann. The wind freshened, and the storm drove Gann and Senganu till they put in at Inber Douglas, where Corcamruad and Corcabaisginn meet.

16. There they landed, and this is the first place to which sheep were brought in Ireland, and Sheep's Height is its flame.

It was on Saturday, the first day of August, that Slainge put into Inber Slainge; Gann and Genann put into Inber Domnann on Friday; and Rudraige and Sengann at Tracht Rudraige on Tuesday. The latter were anxious as to whether the Fir Boig had reached Ireland or not, and sent messengers all over Ireland to gather all of them that had arrived in Ireland to one place, that is, the Stronghold of the Kings in Tara. All of them assembled there. 'We give thanks to the gods,' said they, 'for our return to thee, Ireland. Let the country be divided equitably between us. Bring hither the wise Fintan, and let Ireland be divided according to his decision.'

17. It was then that Fintan made five portions of Ireland. From Inber Colptha to Comar Tri nUisce was given to Slainge, son of Dela, and his thousand men; Gann's portion was from Comar Tri nUisce to Belach Conglais, Sengann's from Belach Conglais to Limerick. Gamin and Sengaun, thus, had the two Munsters. Genann was put over Connacht, and Rudraige over Ulster. The poet describes the division thus:

'On Saturday, an omen of prosperity, Slainge reached lofty Ireland; his bold career began at Inber Slainge.

At dark Inber Douglas the two ships of Sengann and Gann touched the glorious land.

Rudraige and prosperous Genann landed on Friday. These were all of them, and they Were the five kings.

From Inber Colptha to Comar Tri nUisce Fintan made one division; that was the portion of Slainge of the spears. His host was a thousand men.

From Comar Tri nUisce to famous Belach Conglais was the fifth of wound-dealing Gann. He had a following of a thousand men.

To Sengann, methinks, was given from Belach to Limerick. He was at the head of a thousand men when strife threatened.

Genann was undisputed king of Connacht to the Maigue. Heroic Rudraige was king of Ulster; his were two thousand men in the hour of battle.

Rudraige and Sengann of the spears were, it is certain, the chiefs of the Fir Boig. The Gaileon followed glorious Slainge. A good king were he that had a more numerous host. They entered Ireland from the south, as God saw fitting.

18. The wives of these five chiefs were Auaist, Liben, Cnucha, Edar, and Fuat, as the poet says:

'Fuat was the wife of Slainge as you hold, Edar of the warrior Gamin, Auaist of Sengann of the spears, Cnucha of fair Genann.

'Liben was the wife of Rudraige the Red—they made a pleasant company on a visit. However, as for Rudraige, the feat-performing king, I have heard that his wife was Fuat.'

19. The Fir Boig then occupied Ireland, and were masters of it for thirty years.

20. As for the Tuatha De Danann, they prospered till their fame went abroad over the lands of the earth. They had a god of wizardry of their own, Eochaid Ollathir, called the Great Dagda, for he was an excellent god. They had bold, hardy chiefs, and men proficient in every art; and they determined to go to Ireland. Then set out those daring chiefs, representing the military prowess of the world, and the skill and learning of Europe. They came from the northern islands to Dobur and Indobur, to S . . . and Genann's well. There they stayed for four years, and at their coming to Ireland Nuada, son of Echtach, was king over them.

Then those warriors gathered their fleets to one place till they had three hundred ships under way. Thereupon their seers, Cairbre, Aed, and Edan asked the chiefs of the host in which ship they should sail, recommending that of Fiachra. The chiefs approved and went on board. Then they all set sail, and after three years and three days and three nights landed at wide Tracht Mugha in Ulster on Monday of the first week in May.

Now, on the arrival of the Tuatha De Danann in Ireland, a vision was revealed in a dream to Eochaid, son of Erc, high king of Ireland. He pondered over it with much anxiety, being filled with wonder and perplexity. He told his wizard, Cesard, that he had seen, a vision. 'What was the vision?' asked Cesard. 'I saw a great flock of black birds,' said the king, 'coming from the depths of the Ocean. They settled over all of us, and fought with the people of Ireland. They brought confusion on us, and destroyed us. One of us, methought, struck the noblest of the birds and cut off one of its wings. And now, Cesard, employ your skill and knowledge, and tell us the meaning of the vision.' Cesard did so, and by means of ritual and the use of his science the meaning of the king's vision was revealed to him; and he said:

'I have tidings for you: warriors are coming across the sea, a thousand heroes covering the ocean; speckled ships will press in upon us; all kinds of death they announce, a people skilled in every art, a magic spell; an evil spirit will come upon you, signs to lead you astray (?); . . . they will be victorious in every stress.'

21. 'That,' said Eochaid, 'is a prophecy of the coming to Ireland of enemies from far distant countries.'

22. As for the Tuatha De Danann, they all arrived in Ireland, and immediately broke and burnt all their ships and boats. Then they proceeded to the Red Hills of Rian in Brefne in the east of Connacht, where they halted and encamped. And at last their hearts and minds were filled with contentment that they had attained to the land of their ancestors.

23. Now it was reported to the Fir Bolg that that company had arrived in Ireland. That was the most handsome and delightful company, the fairest of form, the most distinguished in their equipment and apparel, and their skill in music and playing, the most gifted in mind and temperament that ever came to Ireland. That too was the company that was bravest and inspired most horror and fear and dread, for the Tuatha Dé excelled all the peoples of the world in their proficiency in every art.

24. 'It is a great disadvantage to us,' said the Fir Bolg, 'that we should have no knowledge or report of where yon host came from, or where they mean to settle. Let Sreng set out to visit them, for he is big and fierce, and bold to spy on hosts and interview strangers, and uncouth and terrifying to behold.' Thereupon Sreng rose, and took his strong hooked reddish-brown shield, his two thick-shafted javelins, his death-dealing (?) sword, his fine four-cornered helmet and his heavy iron club; and went on his way to the Hill of Rain.

The Tuatha Dé saw a huge fearsome man approaching them. 'Here comes a man all alone,' they said. 'It is for information he comes. Let us send some one to speak with him.'

Then Bres, son of Elatha, went out from the camp to inspect him and parley with him. He carried with him his shield and his sword, and his two great spears. The two men drew near to each other till they were within speaking distance. Each looked keenly at the other without speaking a word. Each was astonished at the other's weapons and appearance; Sreng wondered at the great spears he saw, and rested his shield on the ground before him, so that it protected his face. Bres, too, kept silent and held his shield before him. Then they greeted each other, for they spoke the same language—their origin being the same—and explained to each other as follows who they and their ancestors were:

'My flesh and my tongue were gladdened at your pleasant cheerful language, as you recounted the genealogies from Nemed downwards.

'By origin our two peoples are as brothers; our race and kin are descended from Semeon

'This is the proper time to bear it in mind, if we are, in flesh and blood, of the same distinguished race as you.

'Humble your pride, let your hearts draw nigher, be mindful of your brotherhood, prevent the destruction of your own men.'

'High is our temper, lordly our pride and fierce against our foes; you shall not abate it.

'Should our peoples meet, it will be a gathering where many will be crushed; let him who will bring entertainment, 'tis not he that will amuse them.'

25. 'Remove, your shield from before your body and face,' said Bres, 'that I may be able to give the Tuatha De an account of your appearance.' 'I will do so,' said Sreng, 'for it was for fear of that sharp spear you carry that I placed my shield between us.' Then he raised his shield. 'Strange and venomous,' said Bres, 'are those spears, if the weapons of all of you resemble them. Show me your weapons.' 'I will,' said Sreng; and he thereupon unfastened and uncovered his thick-shafted javelins. 'What do you think of these weapons?' he said. 'I see,' said Bres, 'huge weapons, broad-pointed, stout and heavy, mighty and keen-edged.

'Woe to him whom they should smite, woe to him at whom they shall be flung, against whom they shall be cast; they will be instruments of oppression. Death is in their mighty blows, destruction in but one descent of them; wounds are their hard plying; overwhelming is the horror of them.

26. 'What do you call them?' said Bres. 'Battle javelins are these,' said Sreng. 'They are good weapons,' said Bres, 'bruised bodies they mean, gushing gore, broken bones and shattered shields, sure scars and present plague. Death and eternal blemish they deal, sharp, foe-like, and deadly are your weapons, and there is fury for fratricide in the hearts of the hosts whose weapons they are. Let us make a compact and covenant.' They did so. Each came nigh to the other, and Bres asked: 'Where did you spend last night, Sreng?' 'At the hallowed heart of Ireland, in the Rath of the kings in Tara, where are the kings and princes of the Fir Bolg, and Eochaid, High-king of Ireland. And you, whence come you?' 'From the hill, from the crowded capacious camp yonder on the mountain-slope where are the Tuatha De and Nuada, their king, who came from the north of the world in a cloud of mist and a magic shower to Ireland and the land of the west.' (However, he did not believe that it was thus they came).' It was then Sreng said: 'I have a long journey, and it is time for me to go.' 'Go then,' said Bres, 'and here is one of the two spears I brought with me. Take it as a specimen of the weapons of the Tuatha De.' Sreng gave one of his javelins to Bres as a specimen of the weapons of the Fir Bolg. 'Tell the Fir Bolg,' said Bres, 'that they must give my people either battle or half of Ireland.' 'On my word,' said Sreng, 'I should prefer to give you half of Ireland than to face your weapons.' They parted in peace after making a compact of friendship with each other.

27. Sreng went on his way to Tara. He was asked for tidings of the people he had gone to parley with; and he told his story. 'Stout are their soldiers,' he said, 'manly and masterful their men, bloody and battle-sure their heroes, very great and strong their shields, very sharp and hard of shaft their spears, and hard and broad their blades. Hard it is to fight with them; 'tis better to make a fair division of the land, and to give them half of Ireland as they desire.' 'We will not grant that, indeed,' said the Fir Bolg, 'for if we do, the land will all be theirs.'

28. Bres reached his camp, and was asked for a description of the man he had gone to parley with, and of his weapons. 'A big, powerful, fierce man,' he said, 'with vast, wonderful weapons, truculent and hardy withal, without awe or fear of any man.' The Tuatha De said to each other: 'Let us not stay here, but go to the west of Ireland, to some strong place, and there let us face whomsoever comes. So the host travelled westward over plains and inlets till they came to Mag Nia, and to the end of Black Hill, which is called Sliabh Belgadain. On their arrival there they said: 'This is an excellent place, strong and impregnable. From here let us wage our wars, and make our raids, here let us devise our battles and hostings.' Their camping there is mentioned by the poet in the lines:

'From the Hill of Belgadain to the Mountain—lofty is the mountain round which we wage our contests. From its summit the Tuatha De laid hold of Ireland.'

29. It was then that Badb and Macha and Morrigan went to the Knoll of the Taking of the Hostages, and to the Hill of Summoning of Hosts at Tara, and sent forth magic showers of sorcery and compact clouds of mist and a furious rain of fire, with a downpour of red blood from the air on the warriors' heads; and they allowed the Fir Bolg neither rest nor stay for three days and nights. 'A poor thing,' said the Fir Bolg, 'is the sorcery of our sorcerers that they cannot protect us from the sorcery of the Tuatha De,' 'But we will protect you,' said Fathach, Gnathach, Ingnathach, and Cesard, the sorcerers of the Fir Bolg; and they stayed the sorcery of the Tuatha De.

30. Thereupon the Fir Bolg gathered, and their armies and hosts came to one place of meeting. There met the provincial kings of Ireland. First came Sreng and Semne and Sithbrugh the three sons of Sengann, with the people of the provinces of Curói.' There came too Esca, Econn, and Cirb with the hosts of Conchobar's province; the four Sons of Gann with the hosts of the province of

Eochaid son of Luchta; the four sons of Slainge with the army of the province of the Gaileoin; and Eochaid, the High-king, with the hosts of Connacht. The Fir Bolg, numbering eleven battalions, then marched to the entrance of Mag Nia. The Tuatha De, with seven battalions, took up their position at the western end of the plain. It was then that Nuada proposed to the Tuatha De to send envoys to the Fir Boig: 'They must surrender the half of Ireland, and we shall divide the land between us.' 'Who are to be our envoys?' the people asked. 'Our poets,' said the king, meaning Cairbre, Ai, and Edan.

31. So they set out and came to the tent of Eochaid, the High-king. After they had been presented with gifts, they were asked the reason of their coming. 'This is why we are come,' they said, 'to request the dividing of the land between us, an equitable halving of Ireland.' 'Do the nobles of the Fir Bolg hear that?' said Eochaid. 'We do,' they replied, 'but we shall not grant their request till doomsday.' 'Then,' said the poets, 'when do you mean to give battle?' 'Some delay is called for,' said the Fir Bolg nobles, 'for we shall have to prepare our spears, to mend our mail, to shape our helmets, to sharpen our swords, and to make suitable attire.' There were brought to them men to arrange those things. 'Provide,' said they, 'shields for a tenth, swords for a fifth, and spears for a third part. You must each furnish what we require on either side.' 'We,' said the envoys of the Tuatha De to the Fir Bolg, 'shall have to make your spears, and you must make our javelins.' The Tuatha De were then given hospitality till that was done. (However, though it is said here that the Fir Bolg had no spears, such had been made for Rindal, grandfather of their present king.) So they arranged an armistice till the weapons arrived, till their equipment was ready, and they were prepared for battle.

32. Their druids went back to the Tuatha De and told their story from beginning to end, how the Fir Bolg would not share the land

with them, and refused them favour or friendship. The news filled the Tuatha De with consternation.

33. Thereupon Ruad with twenty-seven of the sons of courageous Mil sped westwards to the end of Mag Nia to offer a hurling contest to the Tuatha De. An equal number came out to meet them. The match began. They dealt many a blow on legs and arms, till their bones were broken and bruised, and fell outstretched on the turf, and the match ended. The Cairn of the Match is the name of the cairn where they met, and Glen Came Aillem the place where they are buried.

34. Ruad turned eastward, and told his tale to Eochaid. The king was glad of the killing of the Tuatha De's young soldiers, and said to Fathach, 'Go to the west, and ask of the nobles of the Tuatha De how the battle is to be fought to-morrow —whether it is to be for one day or for several.' The poet went and put the question to the nobles of the Tuatha De, that is, Nuada, the Dagda and Bres. 'What we propose,' they said, 'is to fight them with equal numbers on both sides.' Fathach went back, and reported to the Fir Bolg the choice of the Tuatha De. The Fir Bolg were depressed, for they disliked the choice of the Tuatha De. They decided to send for Fintan to see if he could give them some counsel. Fintan came to them.

The Fir Bolg had entrenched a great fort. (It was called the Fort of the Packs, from the packs of dogs that preyed on the bodies of the dead after the battle, or the Fort of the Blood Pools, from the pools of gore that surrounded the wounded when the people came to see them.') They made a Well of Healing to heal their warriors from their wounds. This was filled with herbs. Another entrenched fort was made by the Tuatha De. (It was called the Fort of the Onsets, from the onsets directed out of the battle.) They dug a Well of Healing to heal their wounds.

When these works had been finished, Cirb asked: 'Whence come ye, and whither go ye? The care of to-morrow's battle be yours. I will lead the attack with Mogarn and his son Ruad, Laige and his father Senach,' 'We will meet them with four battalions,' was the reply.

35. Six weeks of the summer, half the quarter, had gone on the appointed day of battle. The hosts rose on that day with the first glimmer of sunlight. The painted, perfectly wrought shields were hoisted on the backs of brave warriors, the tough, seasoned spears and battle-javelins were grasped in the right hands of heroes, together with the bright swords that made the duels dazzle with light as the shining sunbeams shimmered on the swords' graven groves. Thus the firm, close-packed companies, moved by the compelling passion of their courageous commanders, advanced towards Mag Nia to give battle to the Tuatha De. It was then that the Fir Bolg poet, Fathach, went forward in front of them to describe their fury and spread the report of it. He had raised up and planted firmly in the midst of the plain a pillar of stone, against which he rested. This was the first pillar set up in the plain, and Fathach's Pillar was its name thenceforth. Then Fathach in utter anguish wept floods of fervent, melancholy tears, and said:

'With what pomp they advance! On Mag Nia they marshal with dauntless might. 'Tis the Tuatha De that advance, and the Fir Bolg of the decorated blades.

'The Red Badb will thank them for the battle-combats I look on. Many will be their gashed bodies in the east after their visit to Mag Tured.

'...will be the host after parting with the warriors I speak of. Many a head shall be severed with vigour and with pomp.'

36. The Tuatha formed a compact, well-armed host, marshalled by fighting warriors and provided with deadly weapons and stout shields. Every one of them pressed on his neighbour with the edge of his shield, the shaft of his spear, or the hilt of his sword, so closely that they wounded each other. The Dagda began the attack on the enemy by cutting his way through them to the west, clearing a path for a hundred and fifty. At the same time Cirb made an onslaught on the Tuatha De, and devastated their ranks, clearing a path for a hundred and fifty through them. The battle continued in a series of combats and duels, till in the space of one day great numbers were destroyed. A duel took place between Aidleo of the Tuatha De and Nertchu of the Fir Bolg. The glued seams of their shields were torn, their swords wrenched from their hilts, and the rivets of their spears loosened. Aidleo fell at the hands of Nertchu.

37. By the close of the day the Tuatha De were defeated and returned to their camp. The Fir Bolg did not pursue them across the battlefield, but returned in good spirits to their own camp. They each brought with them into the presence of their king a stone and a head, and made a great cairn of them. The Tuatha De set up a stone pillar called the Pillar of Aidleo, after the first of them to be killed. Their physicians then assembled. The Fir Bolg too had their physicians brought to them. They brought healing herbs with them, and crushed and scattered them on the surface of the water in the well, so that the precious healing waters became thick and green. Their wounded were put into the well, and immediately came out whole.

38. Next morning Eochaid, the High-king, went to the well all alone to wash his hands. As he was doing so, he saw above him three handsome, haughty armed men. They challenged him to combat. 'Give me time,' said the king, 'to go to fetch my weapons.' 'We will allow not a moment's delay for that; the combat must be now.' While the king was in this difficulty, a young active man appeared between him and his enemies, and

turning to the latter, said: 'You shall have combat from me in place of the king.' They raised their hands simultaneously, and fought till all four fell together. The Fir Bolg came up after the struggle was over. They saw the dead men, and the king told them how they had come upon him, and how the solitary champion had fought with them in his stead. The Fir Bolg brought each man a stone to the well for him, and built a great cairn over him. The Champion's Cairn is the name of the cairn, and the hill is called the Hill of the Three. The strangers were Oll, Forus, and Fir, three physicians, brothers of Diancecht, and they had come to spy upon the physicians of the Fir Bolg, when they came upon Eochaid alone washing his face.

39. The battalions of the Tuatha De were straightway drawn up in the plain to the east; and the Fir Bolg came into the plain against them from the west. The chiefs who went out in front of the Tuatha De on that day were Ogma, Midir, Bodb Derg, Diancecht, and Aengaba of Norway. The women, Badb, Macha, Morrigan and Danann offered to accompany them. Against them came of the Fir Bolg, Mella, Ese, Ferb, and Faebur, all sons of Slainge. Strong, mighty blows were dealt by the battalions on either side, and the bosses of shields were broken as they vigorously parried the blows, while the men-at-arms showed their fury, and the warriors their courage. Their spears were twisted by the continual smiting; in the hand-to-hand combats the swords broke on splintered bones; the fearsome battle-cries of the veterans were drowned in the multitude of shouts.

Briskly the young men turned about for the number of the exploits around them on every side. The warriors blenched at the clashing of swords, at the height of the heaving, and the fury of the fall. Well-timed was the warding there, and gallant the guarding, and rapid the rending blows. Nemed, Badrai's son, approached the flank of the Fir Bolg. Then men closed round him, and in the conflict Eochaid's son, Slainge the Fair, made towards him. The two warriors attacked each other. There was

19

straining of spears and shivering of swords and shattering of shields and battering of bodies. However, Nemed fell at the hands of Slainge; they dug his grave and erected a pillar for him, and the Stone of Nemed is its name to this day. Four sons of Slainge, son of Dela, urged the fight against the Tuatha De. On the side of the Tuatha De the four sons of Cencal battled with them. They harassed each other till the sons of Cencal fell before the sons of Slainge. The latter were then set on by the five sons of Lodan the Swift, and the five sons of Lodan fell at their hands. Aengaba of Norway began to mow down the enemy and confuse their ranks. Ruad heard this, and rushed into the fray. The three sons of Dolad met him, and he wreaked his anger on them and they fell before him. From another quarter of the battle the three sons of Telle met him, and were slain by him in the same way. Lamh Redolam and Cosar Conaire were killed by Slainge the Fair by the side of the lake. Of those seventeen the gravestones were planted by the side of the lake, for they had been driven back as far as the lake.

40. Ruad and Aengaba of Norway met; they raised their shields against each other, and kept wounding each other till Aengaba had twenty-four wounds inflicted on him by Ruad. In the end Ruad cut off his head,' and after that went on fighting till nightfall.

41. Ogma, son of Ethliu, made an attack on the host, and his track was marked by pools of crimson blood. From the east side Cirb entered the fray and made an onslaught on the hosts, and three hundred of the Tuatha Dc fell before him.

42. When night fell the Fir Bolg were driven across the battlefield. However, they brought each a head and a stone to Eochaid their king. 'Is it you that have been beaten today?' said the king. 'Yes,' said Cirb; 'but that will not profit them.'

43. Next day it was the turn of Sreng, Semne, and Sithbrug, along with Cirb, to lead the Fir Bolg. They rose early in the morning. A flashing penthouse of shields and a thick forest of javelins they made over them, and the battle-props then moved forward. The Tuatha De saw the Fir Bolg approaching them in that fashion across the plain from the east. 'With how much pomp,' they said, 'do those battle-props enter the plain and draw towards us.' And it was then that the plain got its name of Mag Tured, the Plain of Props.

44. The Tuatha De asked who should lead them on that day. 'I will,' said the Dagda, 'for in me you have an excellent god;' and, thereupon, he went forth with his sons and brothers. The Fir Bolg had firmly stationed their props and columns, and marshalled their battalions on the level of Mag Nia (which, henceforth, was called Mag Tured, the Plain of Props). Each side then sprang at the other. Sreng, son of Sengann, began to dislodge the hosts of the enemy. The Dagda set to breaking the battalions and harrying the hosts and dislodging divisions and forcing them from their positions. Cirb, son of Buan, entered the fray from the east and slaughtered brave men and spirited soldiers. The Dagda heard Cirb's onset, and Cirb heard the Dagda's battering blows. They sprang each at the other. Furious was the fight as the good swords fenced, heroic the heroes as they steadied the infantry, and answered the onslaughts. At last Cirb fell before the Dagda's battering blows.

Sreng, Sengann's son, was pressing back the hosts from their places when he came on three sons of Cairbre Cas of the Tuatha De, and the three sons of Ordan. Cairbre's sons with their three columns fell before the sons of Ordan, as Sreng drove in the hosts. The enemy fell before him on every side, and the fury of the combat grew behind hint

45. After the fall of Cirb the Fir Bolg were driven into their camp. The Tuatha De did not pursue them across the battlefield, but

they took with them a head and a stone pillar apiece including the head of Cirb, which was buried in the Cairn of Cirb's Head.

46. The Fir Bolg were neither happy nor cheerful that night, and as for the Tuatha De, they were sad and dispirited. But during the same night Fintan came with his sons to join the Fir Bolg, and this made them all glad, for valiant were both he and they.

47. In this cheerful mood the morning found them. The signals of their chiefs roused them on the spacious slopes of their camping-ground, and they began to hearten each other to meet danger and peril. Eochaid, the High-king, with his son, Slainge the Fair, and the soldiers and chiefs of Connaught, came forth to join them. Sengann's three sons with the hosts of Curoi's province, took their place at one side of the line. The four sons of Gann with the warriors of Eochaid's province marched to the centre of the same army. Buan's sons Esca and Egconn ranged themselves with the men of Conchobar's province on the other wing. The four sons of Slainge with the host of the Gaileoin brought up the rear of the army. Round Eochaid, the High-king, they made a fold of valour of battle-scarred, blood-becrimsoned braves, and juggling jousters, and the world's trustiest troops. The thirteen sons of Fintan, men proven in courageous endurance of conflict, were brought to where the king was. A flaming mass was the battle on that day, full of changing colours, many feats and gory hands, of sword-play and single combats, of spears and cruel swords and javelins; fierce it was and pitiless and terrible, hard-packed and close-knit, furious and far-flung, ebbing and flowing with many adventures. The Fir Bolg, in the order told, marched boldly and victoriously straight westwards to the end of Mag Tured till they came to the firm pillars and props of valour between themselves and the Tuatha De. The passionate Tuatha De made an impetuous, furious charge in close-knit companies with their venomous weapons; and they formed one mighty gory phalanx under the shelter of red-rimmed, emblazoned, plated, strong shields. The warriors began the conflict. The flanks and

the wings of the van were filled with grey-haired veterans swift to wound; aged men were stationed to assist and attend on the movements of those veterans; and next to those steady, venomous fighters were placed young men under arms. The champions and serving men were posted in the rear of the youths. Their seers and wise men stationed themselves on pillars and points of vantage, plying their sorcery, while the poets took count of the feats and wrote down tales of them. As for Nuada, he was in the centre of the fight. Round him gathered his princes and supporting warriors, with the twelve sons of Gabran from Scythia, his body-guard. They were Tolc, Trenfer, Trenmiled, Garb, Glacedh, Gruasailt Duirdri, Fonnam, Foirisem, Teidm, Tinnargain and Tescad. He would have no joy of life on whom they made a gory wound. ('Twas they that killed the sons of Fintan, and the sons of Fintan killed them.) Thus they delivered their assault after fastening their bodies to rough-edged stones with clasps of iron; and made their way to the place appointed for the battle. At that moment Fathach, the poet of the Fir Bolg, came to his own pillar, and as he surveyed the armies to the east and west, said:

'Swiftly advance the hosts marshalling on Mag Nia their resistless might; 'tis the Tuatha De that advance and the Fir Bolg of the speckled swords.

'Methinks the Fir Boig will lose some of their brothers there— many will be the bodies and heads and gashed flanks on the plain.

'But though they fall on every side (?), fierce and keen will be their onset; though they fall, they will make others to fall, and heroes will be laid low by their impetuous valour.

'Thou hast subdued (?) the Fir Bolg; they will fall there by the side of their shields and their blades; I will not trust to the strength of any one so long as I shall be in stormy Ireland.

I am Fathach, the poet; strongly has sorrow vanquished me, and now, that the Fir Bolg are gone, I shall surrender to the swift advance of disaster.'

48. The furies and monsters and hags of doom cried aloud so that their voices were heard in the rocks 'and waterfalls and in the hollows of the earth. It was like the fearful agonising cry on the last dreadful day when the human race will part from all in this world. In the van of the Tuatha De advanced the Dagda, Ogma, Alla, Bres, and Delbaeth, the five sons of Elatha, together with Bres, grandson of Net, the Fomorian, Aengus, Aed, Cermad the Fair, Midir, Bodb Derg, Sigmall Abartach, Nuada the High-king, Brian, Iuchar and Iucharba, the three sons of Turenn Bigrenn, Cu, Cian and Cethenn, the three sons of Cainte, Goibnenn the Smith, Lucraidh the Joiner, Credne the Craftsman, Diancecht the Physician, Aengaba of Norway, the three queens, Ere, Fotla and Banba, and the three sorceresses, Badb, Macha and Morigan, with Bechuille and Danann their two foster-mothers. They fixed their pillars in the ground to prevent any one fleeing till the stones should flee. They lunged at each other with their keen sharp spears, till the stout shafts were twisted through the quivering of the victims on their points. The edges of the swords turned on the lime-covered shields. The curved blades were tempered in boiling pools of blood in the thighs of warriors. Loud was the singing of the lances as they cleft the shields, loud the noise and din of the fighters as they battered bodies and broke bones in the rear. Boiling streams of blood took the sight from the grey eyes of resolute warriors. It was then that Bres made an onset on the Fir Bolg army, and killed one hundred and fifty of them. He struck nine blows on the shield of Eochaid the High-king, and Eochaid, in his turn, dealt him nine wounds. Sengann's son, Sreng, turned his face to the army of the Tuatha De, and slew one hundred and fifty of them. He struck nine blows on the shield of the High-king Nuada, and Nuada dealt him nine wounds.

Each dealt dire blows of doom, making great gory wounds on the flesh of the other, till under their grooved blades shields and spears, heads and helmets broke like the brittle branches hacked with hatchets wielded by the stout arms of woodsmen. Heroes swayed to this side and that, each circling the other as they sought opportunity for a blow. The battle champions rose again over the rims of their emblazoned shields. Their courage grew, and the valiant virulent men became steadfast as an arch. Their hands shot up with their swords, and they fenced swiftly about the heads of warriors, hacking their helmets. For a moment they thrust back the ranks of the enemy from their places, and at the sight of them the hosts wavered like the water flung far over its sides by a kettle through excess of boiling, or the flood that, like a water-fall, an army splashes up over a river's banks, making it passable for their troops behind them. So a suitable space was cleared for the chiefs; the heroes yielded them their places, and agile combatants their stations; warriors were dislodged by them, and the serving-men fled for horror of them. To them was left the battle. Heavily the earth was trodden under their feet till the hard turf grew soft beneath them. Each of them inflicted thirty wounds on the other. Sreng dealt a blow with his sword at Nuada, and, cutting away the rim of his shield, severed his right arm at the shoulder; and the king's arm with a third of his shield fell to the ground. It was then that the High-king called aloud for help, and Aengaba of Norway, hearing him, entered the fray to protect him. Fierce and furious was the attack Aengaba and Sreng made on each other. Each inflicted on his opponent an equal number of wounds, but they were not comparable as an exchange, for the broad blade of Sreng's lance and his stout spear-shaft dealt deeper, deadlier sounds. As soon as the Dagda heard the music of the swords in the battle-stress, he hastened to the place of conflict with deliberate bounds, like the rush of a great waterfall. Sreng declined a contest with the two warriors; and though Aengaba of Norway did not fall there, it was from the violence of that conflict that he afterwards died. The Dagda came and stood over Nuada, and, after the Tuatha De had taken counsel, he brought

25

fifty soldiers, with their physicians. They carried Nuada from the field. His hand was raised in the king's stead on the fold of valour, a fold of stones surrounding the king,' and on it the blood of Nuada's hand trickled.

49. The Tuatha De maintained the conflict keenly and stoutly, after their king was gone. Bres made his way into the ranks of the Fir Bolg to avenge his king, and came to the spot where Eochaid was urging the battle, and fortifying his fighters and exhorting his heroes and encouraging his captains and arranging his combats. Each of them then made for his opponent, and wounds were inflicted where they were undefended. Before the fierceness of their fury and the weight of their blows, soldiers were thrown into confusion. At last Bres was slain by Eochaid; and the Dagda, Ogma, Alla and Delbaeth attacked the latter to avenge their brother. Eochaid was urging the fight, collecting and encouraging his captains, making close and compact the ranks of the soldiery, holding his fighting men firm and steadfast. The four brothers, in their search for Eochaid, drove the hosts before them to the place where they heard him urging the fight. Mella, Ese, Ferb and Faebur, sons of Slainge, met them and each struck at the other's shield. Their swords clashed and the conflict grew, and the edges of the curved blades cut gory wounds. The four sons of Slainge fell before the other four; and the Gravestones of Slainge's sons is the name of the place where they were buried. The four sons of Gann then entered the fray. Against them advanced Goibnenn the Smith, Lucraid the Joiner, Dian Cecht and Aengaba of Norway. Horrible was the noise made by the deadly weapons in the champions' hands. Those combatants maintained the fight till the four sons of Gann were slain; and the Mound of the Sons of Gann is the name of the place where they were buried.

50. Bedg, Redg and Rinne, the three sons of Ordan, set on the Tuatha De, and the ranks shook before their onset. The three sons of Cainte met them, but they wearied of the fray; and the Mound of the Wizards is the place where they were buried.

51. Brian, Iuchar and Iucharba, the three sons of Turenn Bigrenn, set on the Fir Bolg host. They were opposed by two sons of Buan, and Cairbre son of Den. The sons of Buan were overcome by the sons of Turenn Bigrenn, and the Gravestones of Buan are the gravestones that cover them, and Cairbre's tomb is beside the gravestones.

52. Eochaid and his son, Slainge the Fair, now joined in the fray, and destroyed innumerable companies of the Tuatha De. 'Our best men,' said Eochaid, 'have been destroyed, our people slaughtered, and it befits us to acquit us valorously.' So they made their way across the battlefield once again, and mowed down men and slaughtered soldiers and hacked hosts, and confused the ranks with their onsets. After this long-continued effort Eochaid was overcome by great weariness and excess of thirst. 'Bring Sreng to me,' he said. That was done. 'You and Slainge the Fair,' said Eochaid, 'must maintain the fight till I go in search of a drink, and to bathe my face, for I cannot endure this consuming thirst.' 'It shall be maintained right well,' said Slainge, 'though we are but few to wage it in your absence.' Eochaid then went out of the battle with a guard of one hundred of his soldiers. The Tuatha De followed them, and shouted at them.

53. But Slainge the Fair advanced to meet the host, and offered them battle, and prevented them from following the High-king. He was attacked by powerful Lugaid, son of Nuada, and the two fought a cruel, fierce, strenuous fight, in which there were wounds and bruises and gory gashing. As soon as the rest saw that Slainge was prevailing they gave their support to Lugaid. Lugaid and Slainge fell together; and Lugaid's Grave is the place where Lugaid was buried, and Slainge's Mound the mound where they buried Slainge.

54. When the Tuatha De wizards saw how the king of Ireland was suffering from a burning thirst, they hid from him all the streams and rivers of Ireland till he came to the strand of Eothail.

27

Three sons of Nemed, son of Badrai, followed him, with a hundred and fifty men. They fought on the strand, and a number fell on either side. Eochaid and the sons of Nemed met in combat. Venomous in battle were the sons of Nemed, and tried in fighting against odds was Eochaid. They fought till their bodies were torn and their chests cut open with the mighty onslaughts. Irresistible was the king's onset as he ceaselessly cut down his opponents, till he and the three sons of Nemed fell. Eochaid's Cairn is the cairn where Eochaid was buried (it is also called the Cairn of Eothail), and the Gravestones of the Sons of Nemed are at the western end of the strand.

55. As for Sreng, son of Sengann, he continued fighting for a day and a night after his fellows, till in the end neither side was capable of attacking the other. Their swift blows had grown feeble through all the slaughter and their spirits had fallen through all their ills, and their courage faint through the vastness of their disasters; and so they parted. The Tuatha De retired to the fastness of Cenn Slebe and to the sloping Glen of Blood, and to the Mound of Tears. There the Dagda said:

'Soldiers slain without measure, many a wound on heroes; cruel swords have torn your bodies. The Fir Bolg have overcome you (?) . . . about their lands.'

56. 'What have been your losses in this last battle?' said Nuada to the Dagda. The Dagda told him in these words:

'I will tell, noble Nuada, the tales of the dread battle, and, after that, its calamities and disasters I will tell, O son of Echtach.

'In it fell our nobles before the violence of the Fir Bolg; so great are our losses that few know of them.

'Bres, son of Elatha, a warrior like a tower, attacked the ranks of the Fir Bolg, a glorious fight, and killed one hundred and fifty of them.

'He dealt nine blows—savage was the deed—on the broad shield of Eochaid, and Eochaid dealt Bres nine blows.

'Huge Sreng came and slew three hundred of our host. He dealt nine blows on your shield, Nuada,

'You, Nuada, coolly dealt Sreng nine mighty blows, but Sreng cut off your right arm, impetuous hero, at the shoulder.

'You raised a loud cry for help, and he of Norway came up. Sreng and Aengaba fought with a will a well-contested fight of clashing weapons.

'As Aengaba cried for help, I came up speedily; when I arrived, still unweary, Sreng refused a contest with both of us.

'Mella, Ese, Ferb and blood-red Faebur fell before us in the same battle.

'The four sons of Gann fell at the hands of Goibnenn the Smith, of Aengaba of the exploits, of Lucraidh and of Diancecht.

'Bedg and Rinde and Redg, the three Sons of Ordan of the crafts, were slain surely by the fair sons of Cainte.

'Eochaid and his son, Slainge the Fair, slew in the battle a great number of the heroes of the Tuatha De.

'In the battle thirst overcame king Eochaid, and he got not the draught he sought till he came to the Strand of Eothail.

'The three sons of Nemid overtook him on the silent strand, and there they fought till they all fell together.

'Lugaid, Nuada's son, methinks, was slain by Slainge the Fair; and Slainge, though so fierce before, was killed in fighting with the Tuatha De.

'Brian, Iucharba and Iuchar, the three sons of Turenu Bigrenn, slew Esca and Econn and Airbe.

'After that 'twas Sreng that ruled the fight—and many were those that changed colour—for three days, but neither he nor we turned in the struggle.

'Weary were we now on either side, and we resolved to separate. Each man's combats, as I heard, so shall I exactly tell of.'

57. Sad and weary, wounded and full of heavy reproaches were the Fir Bolg that night. Each one buried his kinsfolk and relatives, his friends and familiars and foster-brothers; and then were raised mounds over the brave men, and gravestones over the warriors, and tombs over the soldiers, and hills over the heroes, After that Sreng, Semne and Sithbrug, the sons of Sengann, called a meeting for council and deliberation to which three hundred assembled. They considered what it was their interest to do, whether they should leave Ireland, or offer regular battle, or undertake to share the land with the Tuatha De. They decided to offer the Tuatha Dc battle, and Sreng said:

'Resistance is destruction for men; we resolutely gave battle; there was clashing of hard swords; the strong plying of spears on the sides of noble warriors, and the breaking of buckler on shield; full of trouble are. the plains of Ireland; disaster we found about its woods, the loss of many good men.'

58. They took up their strong, hooked shields, their venomous spears and their sharp swords with blue blades. Thus equipped they made a keen, murderous charge, a wild fiery company, with their spears close-pressed in the onset, cutting their way in a flaming fire of fury to meet any hardship and any tribulation. It was then that Sreng challenged Nuada to single combat, as they had fought in the previous battle. Nuada faced him bravely and boldly as if he had been whole, and said: 'If single combat on fair terms be what you seek, fasten your right hand, as I have lost mine; only so can our combat be fair.' 'If you have lost your hand, that lays me under no obligations,' said Sreng, 'for our first combat was on fair terms. We ourselves so took up the quarrel.' The Tuatha De took counsel, and their decision was to offer Sreng his choice of the provinces of Ireland, while a compact of peace, goodwill, and friendship should be made between the two peoples. And so they make peace, and Sreng chooses the province of Connacht. The Fir Bolg gathered round him from every side, and stubbornly and triumphantly' took possession of the province against the Tuatha De. The Tuatha De made Bres their king, and he was High-king for seven years. He died after taking a drink while hunting in Sliab Gam, and Nuada, his missing hand having been replaced, became king of Ireland. And that is the story of the battle of Mag Tured Cunga.

This was written in the Plain of Eithne, the Goblin's daughter, by Cormac O'Cuirnin for his companion Sean O'Glaimhmn. Painful to us is his deserting us when he goes from us on a journey.

www.ingramcontent.com/pod-product-compliance
Lightning Source LLC
Chambersburg PA
CBHW070747280626
47162CB00017B/2476